How to Dazzle at
Algebra

Beryl Webber and Jean Haigh

Brilliant
PUBLICATIONS

We hope you and your class enjoy using this book. Other books in the series include:

Maths titles

How to Dazzle at Oral and Mental Starters	978 1 903853 10 8
How to Dazzle at Written Calculations	978 1 903853 11 5
How to Dazzle at Maths Crosswords (Book 1)	978 1 903853 38 2
How to Dazzle at Maths Crosswords (Book 2)	978 1 903853 39 9

English titles

How to Dazzle at Writing	978 1 897675 45 8
How to Dazzle at Reading	978 1 897675 44 1
How to Dazzle at Spelling	978 1 897675 47 2
How to Dazzle at Grammar	978 1 897675 46 5
How to Dazzle at Reading for Meaning	978 1 897675 51 9
How to Dazzle at Macbeth	978 1 897675 93 9
How to Dazzle at Twelfth Night	978 1 903853 34 4
How to Dazzle at Romeo and Juliet	978 1 897675 92 2

Science titles

How to Dazzle at Being a Scientist	978 1 897675 52 6
How to Dazzle at Scientific Enquiry	978 1 903853 15 3

Other titles

How to Dazzle at Information Technology	978 1 897675 67 0
How to Dazzle at Beginning Mapskills	978 1 903853 58 0

To find out more details on any of our resources, please log onto our website: www.brilliantpublications.co.uk

Published by Brilliant Publications,
Unit 10, Sparrow Hall Farm,
Edlesborough,
Dunstable,
Bedfordshire
LU6 2ES, UK

email: info@brilliantpublications.co.uk
website: www.brilliantpublications.co.uk

General information enquiries:
Tel: 01525 222292

The name Brilliant Publications and the logo are registered trademarks.

Written by Beryl Webber and Jean Haigh
Illustrated by Sue Wollatt of
Graham Cameron Illustrations
Cover illustrated by Pat Murray of
Graham Cameron Illustrations

Printed in the UK.

© Beryl Webber and Jean Haigh 2002
Printed ISBN 978 1 903853 12 2
ebook ISBN   978 0 85747 018 8

First published 2002
Reprinted 2009

10 9 8 7 6 5 4 3 2

The right of Beryl Webber and Jean Haigh to be identified as the authors of this work has been asserted by them in accordance with the Copyright, Designs and Patents Act 1988.

Pages 6–48 may be photocopied by individual teachers for class use, without permission from the publisher and without declaration to the Publishers Licensing Society. The material may not be reproduced in any other form or for any other purpose without the prior permission of the publisher.

Contents

	Page
Introduction	4
How to use the book	5
Make 12	6
Digit quads	7
What could it be?	8
What else could it be?	9
Continuity	10
What's my line? 1	11
What's my line? 2	12
It's magic	13
Inverse operations	14
Find your way back	15
Flow charts	16
More flow charts	17
Factorising to the end 1	18
Factorising to the end 2	19
Associative Law	20
Commutative Law	21
Pyramids	22
Brackets 1	23
Brackets 2	24
Brackets 3	25
Brackets 4	26
Multiplying brackets	27
Word problems	28
Think of a number 1	29
Think of a number 2	30
Puzzle equations 1	31
Puzzle equations 2	32
Arithmogons	33
Different solutions – addition	34
Different solutions – subtraction	35
Different solutions – multiplication	36
Different solutions – division	37
Break the code 1	38
Break the code 2	39
Expressions and equations	40
Graph vocabulary	41
Co-ordinates	42
Graphs 1	43
Graphs 2	44
Graphs 3	45
Investigations	46
Check test 1	47
Check test 2	48

Introduction

How to Dazzle at Algebra contains 43 photocopiable sheets for use with pupils who are working at level 3 of the National Curriculum. The activities are presented in an age-appropriate manner and provide a flexible but structured resource for teaching pupils to develop an understanding of algebra. The book is based on the introduction to the algebra section of the National Numeracy Strategy – *A Framework for Teaching Mathematics from Reception to Year 6* and links with the Year 7 algebra work introduced to pupils in Year 7.

The precise rules and conventions required for the understanding of algebra are emphasized throughout the book. The algebraic ideas are based on forming and solving equations, introduction to inverses, identification of number patterns, graphical representation, continuity, factorising, equivalence, and the laws of arithmetic.

Algebra is for some pupils daunting and for others exciting and viewed as a new challenge. If pupils can feel confident by acquiring the basic skills required to take them into a Key Stage 3 programme, they will be able to progress towards the algebra requirement of the Key Stage 3 SATs without a feeling of failure. Many of these mathematical ideas will have been attempted during Key Stage 2 lessons. These activities will give pupils the opportunity to revisit and explore algebraic ideas in a different setting and focus on specific aspects of the subject.

How to use the book

The activity sheets are designed to supplement any numeracy programme you undertake in the classroom. They are intended to add to the pupils' knowledge of the foundations for algebraic thinking.

The activities give opportunities to try different methods of working. The specific language attached to algebra is linked to the learning objectives for Year 7. Pupils with poor reading skills may need support with the problems. However, they should be able to extract the mathematics themselves and decide on the correct operation to apply. Some of the activities can be used during the main part of the lesson as activities to enable a mixed-ability class to work on a similar theme. The pupils will then be able to interact during the plenary to share what they have been learning.

It is not the intention of the authors that the teacher should expect all the pupils to complete all the sheets, rather that the sheets be used with a flexible approach, so that the book will provide a bank of resources that will meet the needs as they arise.

Many of the sheets can be modified and extended by creating further examples. The Add-ons provide a good vehicle for discussion of what has been learned and how it can be applied. The Add-ons should always be included in any class or group discussion at the end of the lesson or in some cases may be suitable as homework tasks for discussion at a later date.

There are two check tests that involve the algebraic ideas contained in the activity sheets. There are twenty questions in each test, which can be divided into two parts so that you can spend time working with pupils who need help with reading. They contain test items covering all aspects of the algebra covered by the activities in the book. These tests can be used to identify the progress pupils have made in their understanding of the foundations of algebra before embarking on the full Key Stage 3 programme contained in the National Numeracy Strategy.

Make 12

Investigate ways of making 12 using two numbers.

☐ + ☐ = 12

Hint:
Constant means the number always stays the same.

Investigate ways of making 12 holding 4 constant.

△(4) + ☐ + ☐ = 12

Try with a different constant.

△ + ☐ + ☐ = 12

Try with −2 as the constant.

△(−2) + ☐ + ☐ = 12

Try with a different negative number as the constant.

△(−) + ☐ + ☐ = 12

Try with two constants. Make one negative.

△ + △(−) + ☐ + ☐ = 12

Add-on
Investigate ways of making 6 or 24. Is there any relationship to the ways of making 12?

Digit quads

Use the digits in the grids to make the highest and the lowest two-digit numbers possible. Use each digit only once. Then find the difference between them.

				Highest	Lowest	Difference
7	4	9	6	97	46	51
8	1	2	4			
9	3	3	2			
8	5	4	6			
9	7	4	8			
2	0	9	3			
2	1	5	4			
7	3	9	1			
3	6	8	1			

Describe how you did this.

Now use the same grids to make two two-digit numbers with the smallest possible difference.

| 7 | 4 | 9 | 6 | $74 - 69 = 5$

Describe how you did this. Is there a rule?

Add-on
Using any of the digits 0–9, investigate which four digits would have the largest difference and which would have the smallest.

© Beryl Webber and Jean Haigh
This page may be photocopied for use by the purchasing institution only.

How to Dazzle at Algebra

What could it be?

Investigate which numbers can be placed correctly in each box.

Hint:
< means 'is less than'
> means 'is greater than'

1	<	☐	<	10
3	<	☐	<	5
1	<	☐	<	3
1	<	☐	<	2
100	>	☐	>	90
6.5	>	☐	>	6.0
$\frac{1}{2}$	>	☐	>	0

Which is the largest number you can place in each box?

Which is the smallest?

Add-on
Investigate which numbers will go in these boxes.

−1 < ☐ < 1   0.1 < ☐ < 0.2   0.15 < ☐ < 0.2

What else could it be?

Investigate which numbers can be placed correctly in each box.

Hint:
≤ means 'is less than or equal to'
≥ means 'is greater than or equal to'

10	≤	☐	≤	20
10	≤	☐	<	15
1	<	☐	≤	2
0	≥	☐	≥	−5
100	≥	☐	≥	99
0.5	>	☐	≥	0

Which is the largest number you can place in each box?

Which is the smallest?

Add-on
Investigate which numbers could go in these boxes.

1 < ☐ ≤ 2 ≤ ☐ < 3

Continuity

Find a number between these numbers.

1	<	☐	<	2
1	<	☐	<	1.1
1	<	☐	<	1.01
1	<	☐	<	1.001
1	<	☐	<	1.0001
1	<	☐	<	1.00001

You could go on for ever like this! Try these:

−1	<	☐	<	0
−0.1	<	☐	<	0
−0.01	<	☐	<	0

Add-on
Discuss with a friend whether, when the outside temperature drops from 15°C to 10°C, it has been all the temperatures in between at one point.

What's my line? 1

What rule am I using?

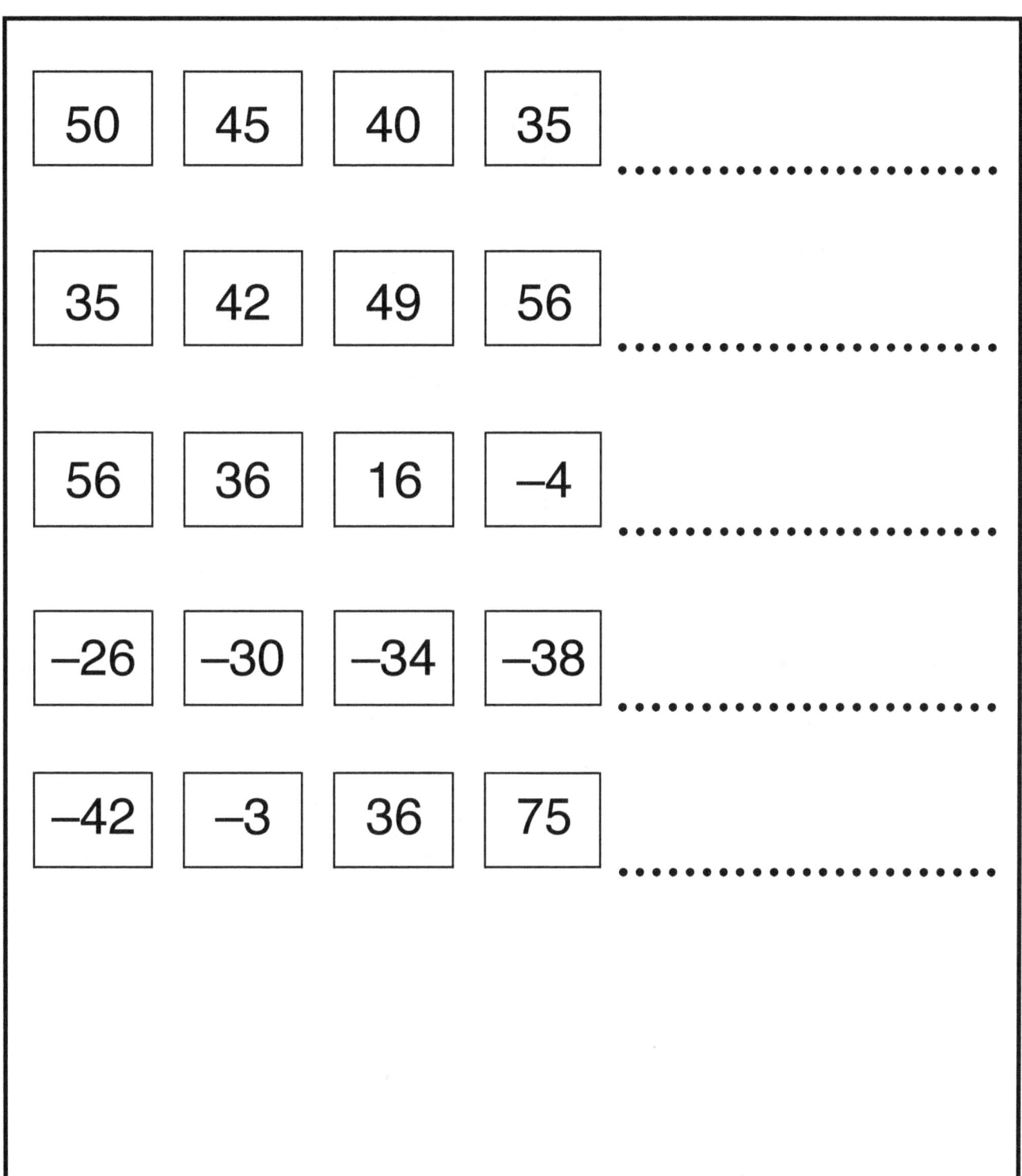

Add-on
Make up some more of your own. See if a friend can find the rule.

What's my line? 2

What rule am I using?

| 100 | 96 | 106 | 102 | 112 | .... |

| 99 | 90 | 91 | 82 | 83 | .... |

| 1.4 | 2.4 | 2.3 | 3.3 | 3.2 | .... |

| –3 | 1 | –4 | 0 | –5 | .... |

| 19 | 28 | 37 | 46 | 54 | .... |

Add-on
Make up some more of your own. See if a friend can find the rule.

It's magic

Ask a friend to follow your instructions:

| Think of a number |
| Add 4 |
| Multiply by 3 |
| Subtract 9 |
| Divide by 3 |
| Tell me your answer |

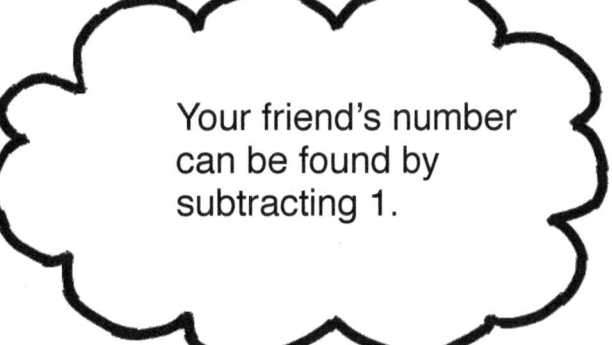

Your friend's number can be found by subtracting 1.

Now try these:

| Think of a number |
| Add 4 |
| Multiply by 8 |
| Subtract 5 |
| Add on your number |
| Divide by 9 |
| Tell me your answer |

| Think of a number |
| Subtract 3 |
| Multiply by 2 |
| Add 2 |
| Divide by 2 |
| Tell me your answer |

What is the relationship between the number you thought of and the final answer in these two examples?

Is it aways the same?

Add-on
See if you can work out how this works.
Make up some more of your own.

Inverse operations

Use these symbols once each to make these equations correct.

$\boxed{+}$ $\boxed{-}$ $\boxed{\times}$ $\boxed{\div}$

---

6 ☐ 2 ☐ 2 ☐ 2 ☐ 2 = 6

7 ☐ 4 ☐ 3 ☐ 3 ☐ 4 = 7

10 ☐ 2 ☐ 3 ☐ 3 ☐ 2 = 10

0.5 ☐ 4 ☐ 5 ☐ 5 ☐ 4 = 0.5

−6 ☐ 1 ☐ 2 ☐ 2 ☐ 1 = −6

3 ☐ 2 ☐ 2 ☐ 5 ☐ 5 = 3

3 ☐ 4 ☐ 2 ☐ 2 ☐ 4 = 3

Now try this one. Use the symbols twice each.

9 ☐ 7 ☐ 6 ☐ 6 ☐ 7 ☐ 3 ☐ 4 ☐ 3 ☐ 4 = 9

How to Dazzle at Algebra

Find your way back

An inverse operation is one which takes you back to the number you started with.

{4} + 3 = 7   so   7 − 3 = {4}

Find the inverses for these calculations:

					Inverse				
12	+	3	=	15	15	−	3	=	12
6	+	2.5	=	8.5					
24	+	3	=	27					
92	+	37	=	129					
68	−	8	=	60					
42	−	12	=	30					
6.03	−	1.15	=	4.88					
12	x	2	=	24					
8	x	6	=	48					
9	x	10	=	90					
0.1	x	15	=	1.5					
42	÷	6	=	7					
1	÷	10	=	0.1					
10	÷	100	=	0.1					

Add-on
Investigate the inverses of mixed calculations such as:
3 + 4 − 2 = 5   6 x 2 − 1 = 11

Flow charts

Which flow charts start and finish with the same numbers?

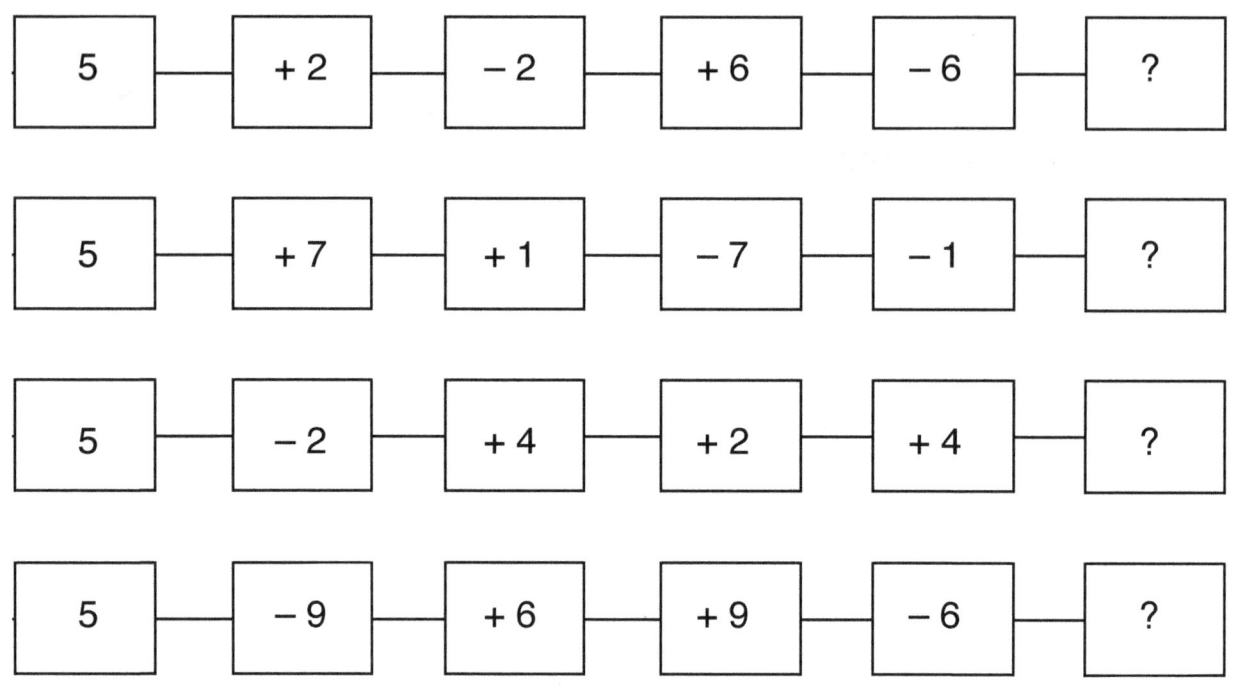

Why?

Make up some flow charts of your own that start and finish with the same number.

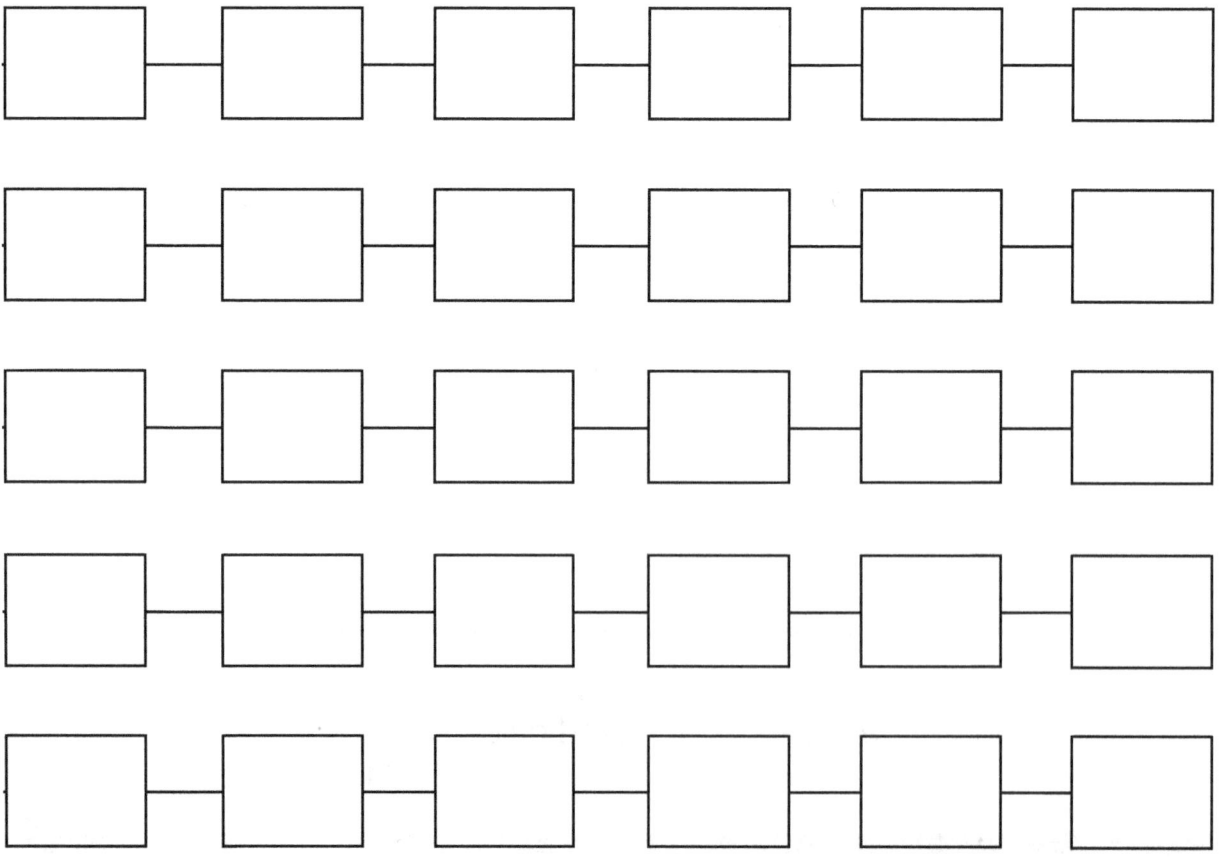

More flow charts

Which flow charts start and finish with the same numbers?

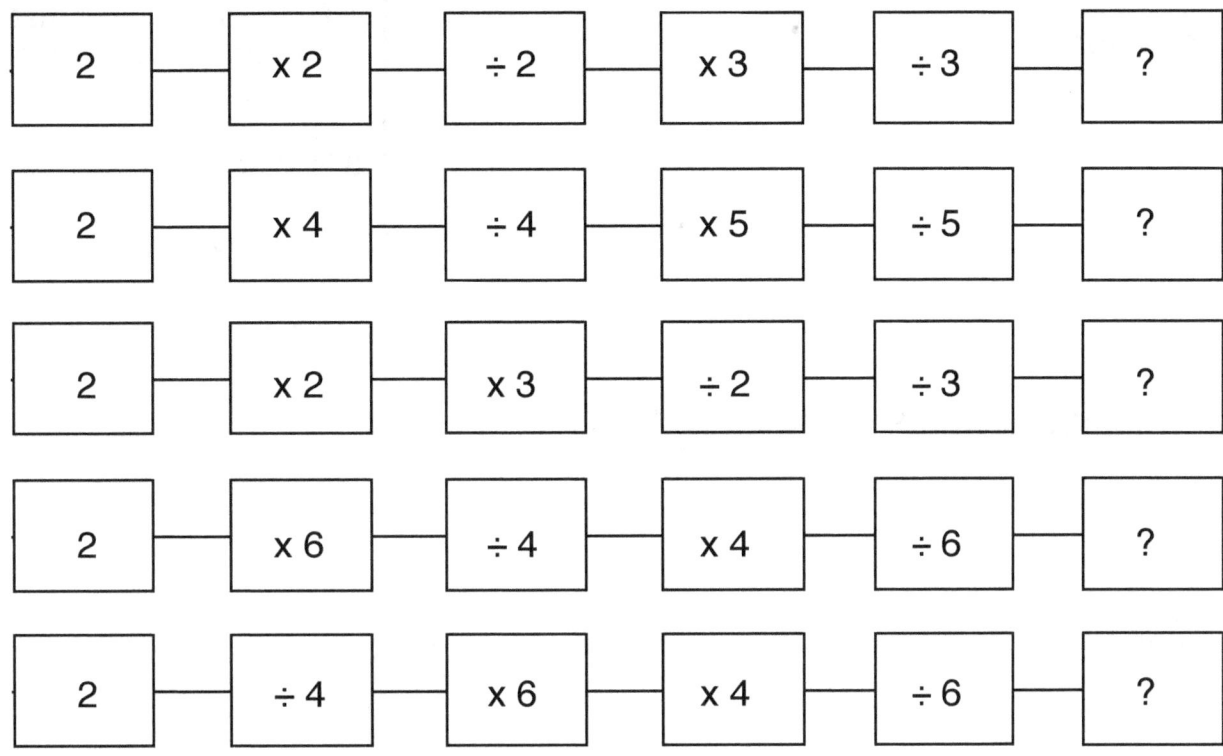

Why?

Make up some flow charts of your own that start and finish with the same number.

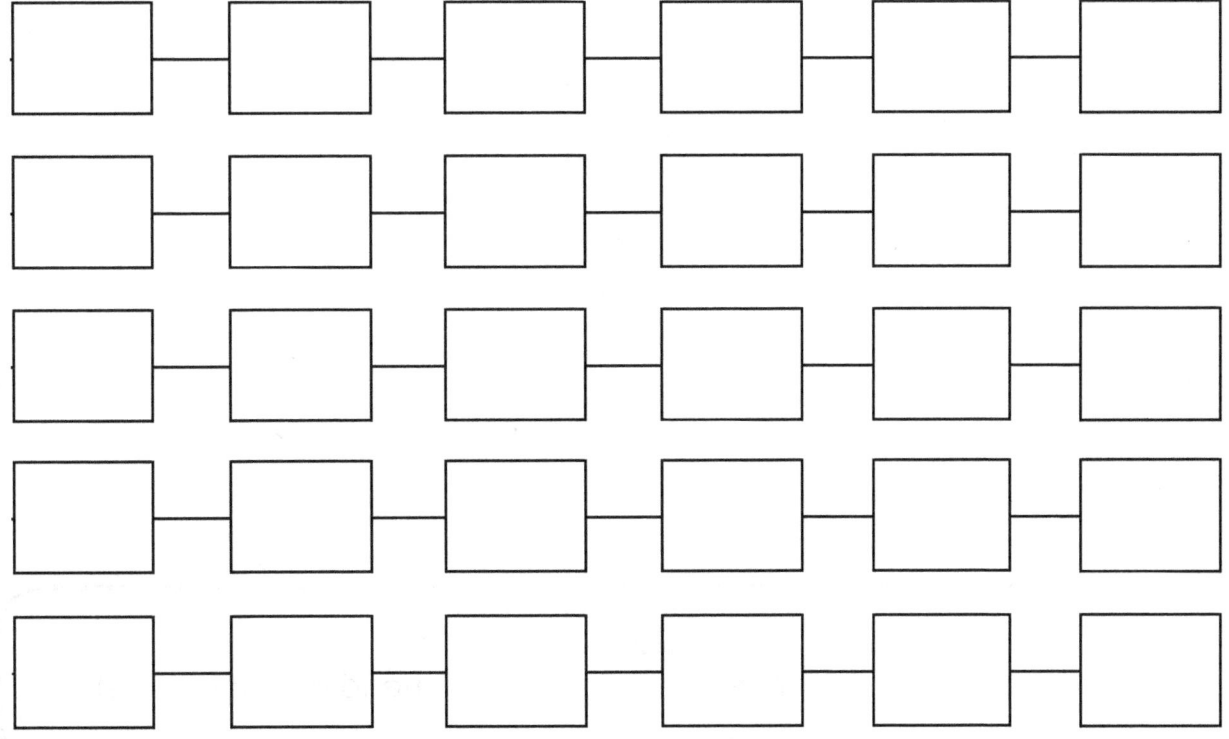

Factorising to the end 1

12 has factors   2 x 6

6 has factors   2 x 3

so 12 has factors   2 x 2 x 3

> **Reminder:**
> A factor is a number that goes exactly into another number.
>
> 3 is a factor of 6 and 12.
>
> 10 has factors of 1, 2, 5 and 10.

Factorise these numbers as far as you can...

Add-on
Find a number with seven factors. See if your friend can find the all.

Factorising to the end 2

Factorise these as far as you can...

180

273

1287

a^2

$3b^3$

$3a + 6$

Add-on
Make up an algebraic expression that has $3x$ as a factor.

Associative Law

The Associative Law applies when numbers can be regrouped without changing their order and the answer is still the same.

For example:

$$4 + 3 + 7 \longrightarrow (4 + 3) + 7 = 4 + (3 + 7)$$
$$7 + 7 = 4 + 10$$

Put a tick (✔) by the calculations that show the Associative Law.

$9 \times 2 \times 3$

$8 + 2 + 1 + 9$

$9 \times 3 - 4 + 6$

$5 + 4 \times 2 + 3$

$8 \times 4 \times 2 \times 3$

$a + b + c$

$a \times b \times c$

$2a - 1 \times a$

Add-on
How can the Associative Law help you to work out calculations?

How to Dazzle at Algebra

Commutative Law

The Commutative Law applies if you can change the order of the numbers in a calculation and you still get the same answer.

Put a tick (✓) by the calculations that show the Commutative Law.

3 + 4   42 ÷ 7

9 − 2   112 x 13

8 x 7   2 x 3 x 5 x 7

12 ÷ 6 $a + b$

5 + 7 + 9 $2m - n$

11 − 3 + 1 $3d$ x a

Add-on
Describe situations when the Commutative Law applies and when it doesn't. How does it help when doing calculations?

Pyramids

Number pyramids are formed by adding adjacent numbers to get the number above.

Hint:
Make the expressions as simple as possible.

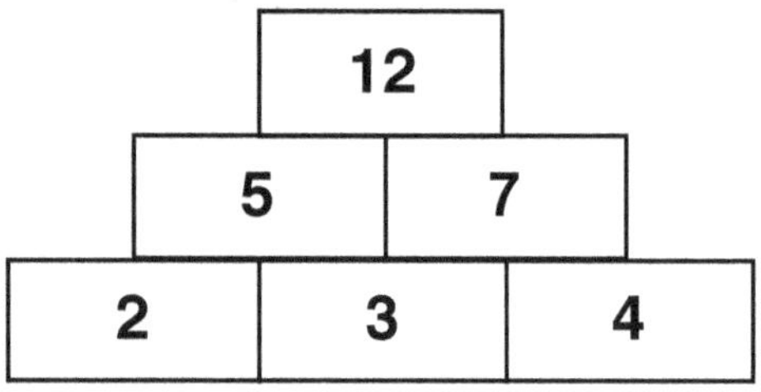

Complete these pyramids.

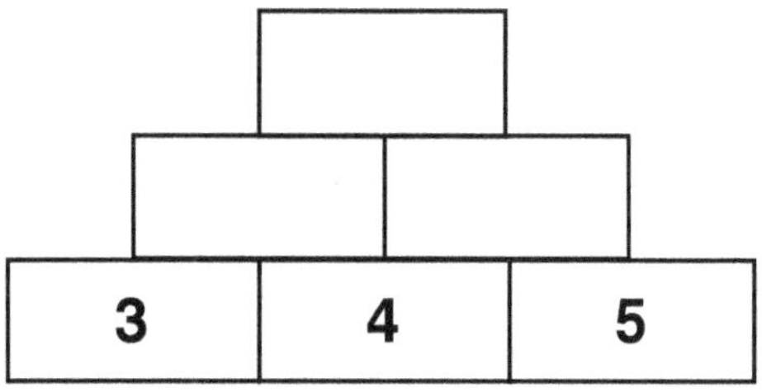

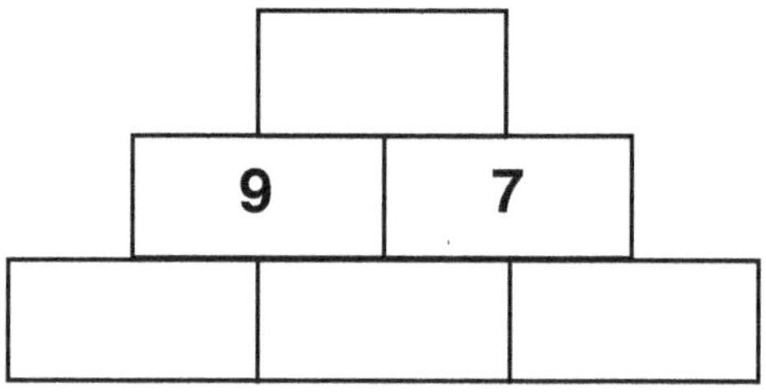

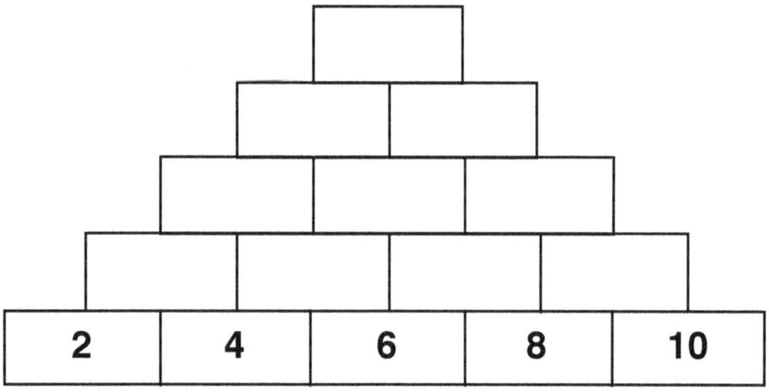

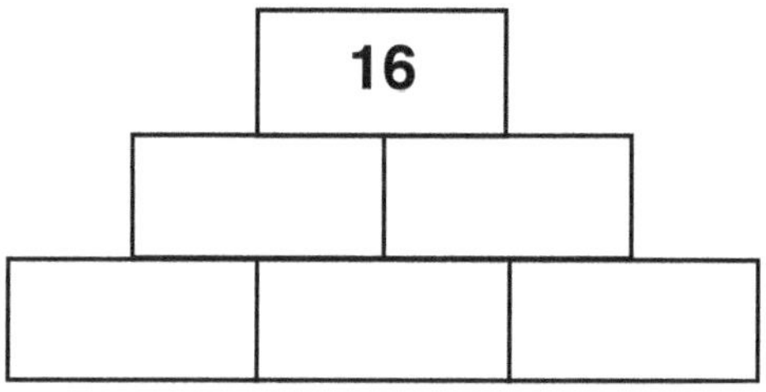

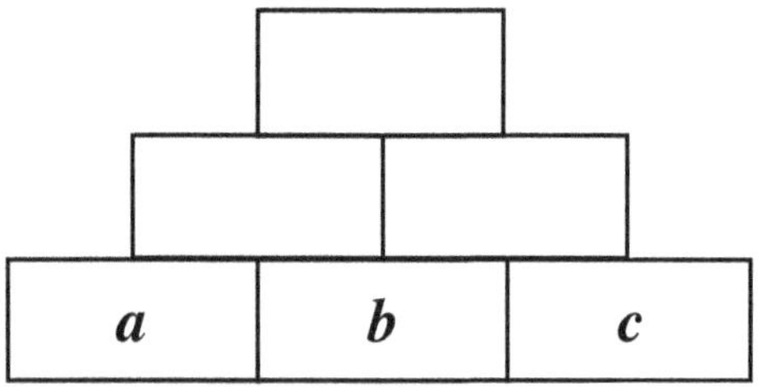

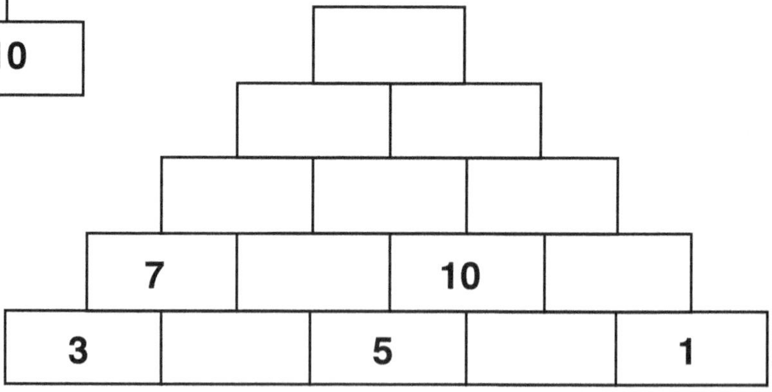

Add-on

Complete this pyramid.
What is the value of x?

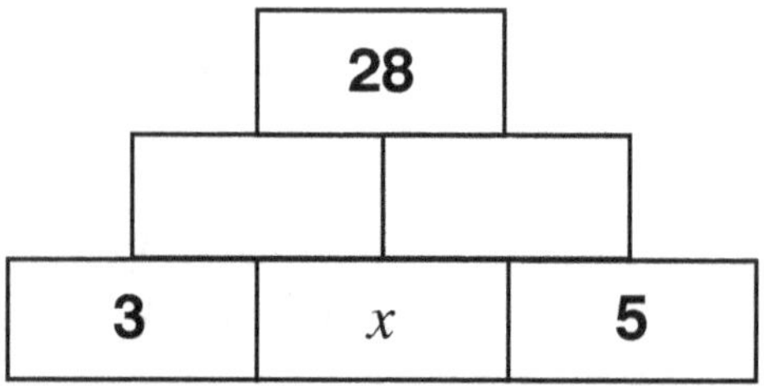

Brackets 1

You must remember to multiply before you add or subtract.

For example: 5 + 2 x 3   =   5 + 6 =   11

Note: Brackets mean 'do this first'.

Try these calculations.

3 + 2 x 4

4 x 3 + 2

8 − 3 x 2

2 x 8 − 3

Now try them with brackets. Is there any difference?

(3 + 2) x 4

4 x (3 + 2)

(8 − 3) x 2

2 x (8 − 3)

When using brackets you don't have to use the multiplication sign, so 3 x (6 + 1) is the same as
   3(6 + 1)

Rewrite the calculations above without the multiplication sign. What do you notice?

Add-on
Investigate putting brackets in this calculation:
4 + 2 − 3 x 6 + 4 x 3 − 1 + 2 x 2 =

Brackets 2

There are two ways to multiply out brackets.

1. 3(2 + 4) = 3 x 6   (work out the bracket first and then multiply)

2. 3(2 + 4) = 6 + 12   (multiply each number in the bracket by the one outside then add)

Try these:

	Method 1	Method 2
2(3 + 4)	2 x 7 = 14	6 + 8 = 14
6(9 + 7)		
0.5(1 + 2)		
−3(2 + 9)		
6(9 − 4)		
10(3 − 1)		
1.5(2.7 − 0.2)		
$\frac{1}{2}$(3 − 1)		
9(6 + 4)		
$a(b + c)$		
$x(z − y)$		
3($a + b$)		

Add-on
Investigate ways of multiplying out
(2 + 3)(4 + 1) or (2 + 4)(8 − 6)

Brackets 3

There are two ways of multiplying out two pairs of brackets.

1. (2 + 1)(3 + 4) = 3 x 7   (work out the brackets first then multiply)

2. (2 + 1)(3 + 4) = 6 + 8 + 3 + 4   (multiply each number in the second bracket by each number in the first)

Try these:

	Method 1	Method 2
(3 + 2)(4 + 5)	5 x 9 = 45	12 + 15 + 8 + 10 = 45
(3 + 1)(2 + 3)	4 x 5 = 20	6 + 9 + 2 + 3 = 20
(6 + 7)(5 + 3)	13 x 8 = 104	30 + 18 + 35 + 21 = 104
(4 + 3)(2 + 7)	7 x 9 = 63	8 + 28 + 6 + 21 = 63
(3 + 4)(5 + 6)	7 x 11 = 77	15 + 18 + 20 + 24 = 77
(2 + 6)(10 + 2)	8 x 12 = 96	20 + 4 + 60 + 12 = 96
(8 + 7)(3 + 5)	15 x 8 = 120	24 + 40 + 21 + 35 = 120
(2 + 4)(5 + 3)	6 x 8 = 48	10 + 6 + 20 + 12 = 48
(3 + 3)(2 + 2)	6 x 4 = 24	6 + 6 + 6 + 6 = 24
(7 + 6)(9 + 1)	13 x 10 = 130	63 + 7 + 54 + 6 = 130
(8 + 2)(7 + 3)	10 x 10 = 100	56 + 24 + 14 + 6 = 100
(7 + 3)(2 + 3)	10 x 5 = 50	14 + 21 + 6 + 9 = 50
(8 + 2)(7 + 3)	10 x 10 = 100	56 + 24 + 14 + 6 = 100
(7 + 3)(2 + 3)	10 x 5 = 50	14 + 21 + 6 + 9 = 50
(6 + 3)(a + b)	$9(a+b) = 9a + 9b$	$6a + 6b + 3a + 3b$
(a + b)(c + d)		$ac + ad + bc + bd$

Add-on
Investigate ways of multiplying out (3 + 2)(5 − 1) or (4 − 1)(5 + 3).

Brackets 4

There are two ways of multiplying out two pairs of brackets.

1. $(2 + 1)(6 - 3) = 3 \times 3$ (work out the brackets first then multiply)

2. $(2 + 1)(6 - 3) = 12 - 6 + 6 - 3$ (multiply each number in the second bracket by each number in the first)

Try these:

	Method 1	Method 2
$(5 + 2)(9 - 4)$	$7 \times 5 = 35$	$45 - 20 + 18 - 8 = 35$
$(5 - 2)(6 - 3)$	$3 \times 3 = 9$	$30 - 15 - 12 + 6 = 9$
$(4 + 1)(3 - 1)$		
$(5 - 2)(7 - 5)$		
$(6 + 3)(9 - 4)$		
$(8 - 3)(9 - 2)$		
$(4 - 1)(2 + 3)$		
$(8 - 4)(9 + 2)$		
$(7 + 3)(8 - 1)$		
$(3 + 4)(5 - 2)$		
$(8 + 1)(10 - 7)$		
$(20 - 3)(20 - 2)$		
$(16 - 4)(17 - 3)$		
$(a - b)(c + d)$		
$(a + b)(c - d)$		
$(a - b)(c - d)$		

Add-on
Investigate ways of multiplying out these brackets:

$(a + b)(a - b)$ $(a - b)(a - b)$ $(a + b)(a + b)$

Multiplying brackets

Use a grid to help you multiply these brackets.

For example:

$(4 + 2)(1 + 7)$

$= 4 + 28 + 2 + 14$

$= 48$

	1	7
4	4	28
2	2	14

$(2 + a)(3 + b)$

	3	b
2		
a		

$(a + 2)(a + 4)$

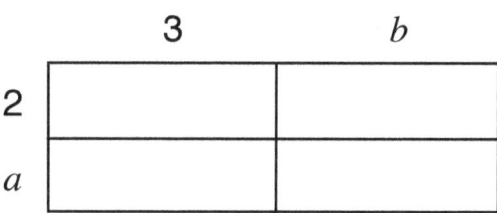

$(2x + 4)(y + 5)$

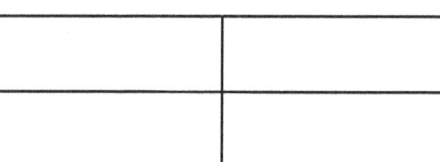

$(a + b)(c + d)$

Add-on
Multiply these brackets using a grid:
$(2x + y + 3)(x + 3y + 5)$

How to Dazzle at Algebra

Word problems

Jessica's brother is 4 years younger than her. If you add their ages together they total 22.

How old is Jessica's brother?

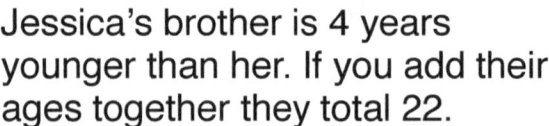

James's sister is twice as old as him. Their ages add up to 36.

How old is James?

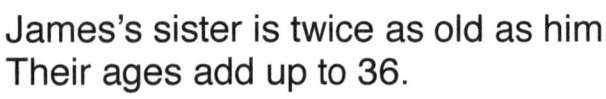

Katy has 4 more CDs than her sister. They have 16 CDs altogether. How many CDs does Katy have?

Add-on
Paul has a paper round. He earns £10 per week.
His friend earns £2 per week washing his dad's car.
Make up a word problem using this information.

Think of a number 1

Example

I think of a number and add 10

| Write the expression | $n + 10$ |

And my answer is 23

| Write the equation | $n + 10 = 23$ |

And my number is:

| Solve the equation | $n = 23 - 10$ |
| | $n = 13$ |

I think of a number and add 57

| Expression |

My answer is 103

| Equation |

My number is

| Solution |

I think of a number and add 7.5

| Expression |

My answer is 29

| Equation |

My number is

| Solution |

Add-on
Make up some more of your own.

Think of a number 2

I think of a number and subtract 15

| Expression |

My answer is 40

| Equation |

My number is

| Solution |

I think of a number and subtract 79

| Expression |

My answer is 183

| Equation |

My number is

| Solution |

I think of a number and subtract 12.25

| Expression |

My answer is 15.75

| Equation |

My number is

| Solution |

Add-on
Can you solve this one? I thought of a number. I multiplied by 2. I subtracted 7 and then multiplied by 3. The answer was 9. What was my number?

Puzzle equations 1

I have two different numbers and they total 10.
When the smaller is subtracted from the larger the difference is 2.
What are my numbers?

$a + b = 10$ $a - b = 2$
                     so $a = 2 + b$
                     so $2 + b + b = 10$
                     so $b = 4$
                     so $a = 6$

Try these:

Total	Difference	a	b
3	1		
8	2		
14	6		
16	2		
36	4		
80	20		
4.5	1.5		
3.5	0.5		
26	12		

Add-on

Try these:

Total	Difference	a	b
2	6		
−4	−2		

Puzzle equations 2

I have two different numbers and they multiply to make 12. When the larger is divided by the smaller the answer is 3. What are my numbers?

$a \times b = 12$ $a \div b = 3$
so $a = b \times 3$
so $b \times 3 \times b = 12$
so $b = 2$
so $a = 6$

Try these:

x	÷	a	b
75	3		
80	5		
24	6		
108	3		
96	6		
20	5		
63	7		
324	4		
1000	10		
405	5		
1331	11		
6.75	1.5		

Add-on

Try these:

x	÷	a	b
−16	−4		
−50	−2		

How to Dazzle at Algebra

Arithmogons

Find the missing numbers in the arithmogons. Remember, the total of the numbers in the circles goes in the square between them.

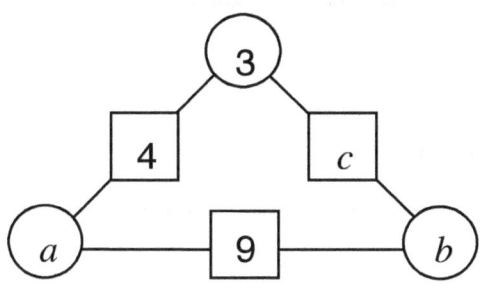

$3 + a = 4$	$1 + b = 9$	$3 + 8 = c$
$a = 1$	$b = 8$	$c = 11$

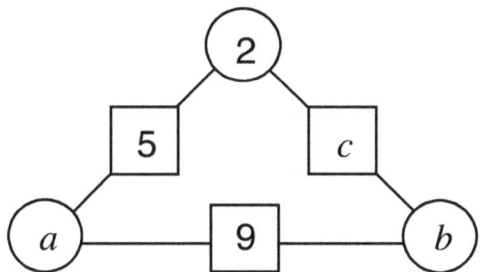

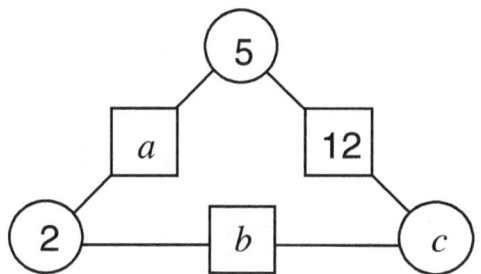

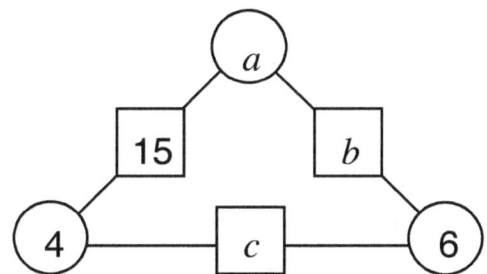

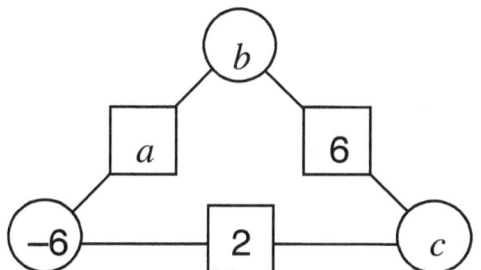

Add-on
Make up some arithmogons for your friend to solve.

Different solutions – addition

Given different parts of an equation, it is possible to work out a range of solutions. The unknown numbers are called variables.

For example: ☐ + ☐ = 20   could be

12 + 8 = 20   11 + 9 = 20   10 + 10 = 20

Try these:

☐ + ☐ = 24   ☐ + ☐ = 73

☐ + ☐ = 105   ☐ + 32 = ☐

☐ + 63 = ☐   ☐ + 123 = ☐

52 + ☐ = ☐   94 + ☐ = ☐

129 + ☐ = ☐

Try some of your own.

☐ + ☐ = ☐   ☐ + ☐ = ☐

☐ + ☐ = ☐

Add-on
Investigate a range of solutions for three variables.

☐ + ☐ + ☐ = ☐

Different solutions – subtraction

Given different parts of an equation, it is possible to work out a range of solutions. The unknown numbers are called variables.

For example: ☐ – ☐ = 20   could be

40 – 20 = 20   30 – 10 = 20   119 – 99 = 20

Try these:

☐ – ☐ = 32   ☐ – ☐ = 75

☐ – ☐ = 107   ☐ – 15 = ☐

☐ – 38 = ☐   ☐ – 126 = ☐

112 – ☐ = ☐   99 – ☐ = ☐

444 – ☐ = ☐

Try some of your own.

☐ – ☐ = ☐   ☐ – ☐ = ☐

☐ – ☐ = ☐

Add-on
Investigate a range of solutions for three variables.

☐ – ☐ – ☐ = ☐

Different solutions – multiplication

Given different parts of an equation, it is possible to work out a range of solutions. The unknown numbers are called variables.

> For example: ☐ x ☐ = 12   could be
>
> 6 x 2 = 12   2 x 6 = 12   3 x 4 = 12   12 x 1 = 12   etc

Try these:

☐ x ☐ = 15   ☐ x ☐ = 63

☐ x ☐ = 100   ☐ x 9 = ☐

☐ x 7 = ☐   ☐ x 8 = ☐

10 x ☐ = ☐   6 x ☐ = ☐

11 x ☐ = ☐

Try some of your own.

☐ x ☐ = ☐   ☐ x ☐ = ☐

☐ x ☐ = ☐

> **Add-on**
> Find some examples of equations where there can only be two whole number variables.

Different solutions – division

Given different parts of an equation, it is possible to work out a range of solutions. The unknown numbers are called variables.

For example: □ ÷ □ = 10   could be

30 ÷ 3 = 10   100 ÷ 10 = 10   5 ÷ 0.5 = 10

Hint: It does not always need to be a whole number.

Try these:

□ ÷ □ = 4

□ ÷ □ = 12

□ ÷ □ = 25

□ ÷ 8 = □

□ ÷ 7 = □

□ ÷ 9 = □

24 ÷ □ = □

72 ÷ □ = □

90 ÷ □ = □

Try some of your own.

□ ÷ □ = □

□ ÷ □ = □

□ ÷ □ = □

Add-on
Find some examples of equations using decimal numbers as the division. For example:

□ ÷ 0.5 = □

Break the code 1

Use these equations to help you solve the code.

$b + 2 = 6$

$f \times 2 = 6$

$5i = 55$

$u + 1 = 9$

$e^2 = 81$

$10t = 50$

$y \div 2 = 3.5$

$m^2 = 1$

$\dfrac{v}{2} + 1 = 4$

$3h + 5 = 35$

$\sqrt{s} = 4$

$2(a + 1) = 26$

$\dfrac{r + 3}{2} = 9$

$p - 7 = -5$

$\dfrac{2(l + 7)}{4} = 10$

| 4 | 8 | 3 | 3 | 7 |

| 5 | 10 | 9 |

| 6 | 12 | 1 | 2 | 11 | 15 | 9 |

| 16 | 13 | 12 | 7 | 9 | 15 |

Break the code 2

Use these equations to help you solve the code.

$$e^3 = 8$$

$$2t^2 - 6 = 44$$

$$\frac{3h}{2} = 10\tfrac{1}{2}$$

$$5m - 4 = 16$$

$$o + 4 = 5$$

$$\frac{6(u+7)}{5} = 12$$

$$2r + 12 = 24$$

$$n = \sqrt{64}$$

$$3a - 1 = 26$$

$$\frac{6}{s} = 0.6$$

$$p + 9 = 8$$

| 5 | 1 | 5 | 5 | 2 | 8 | 7 | 9 | 4 |

| 7 | 1 | 5 | 10 | −1 | 3 | 6 |

Expressions and equations

Sort these into two groups.

$2 + x$ $n - 2$ $\dfrac{x}{2} = 6$

$2n$ $2x = 0.8$ $2(n + 2)$ $\dfrac{2}{x}$

$x + 2 = \frac{1}{2}$

$x - 2 = 15$ $2(n + 2) = 12$

Expressions	Equations

What would you need to know to turn the expressions into equations?

Add-on
Substitute $n = 2$ or $x = 2$ into the expressions.
Solve the equations.

Graph vocabulary

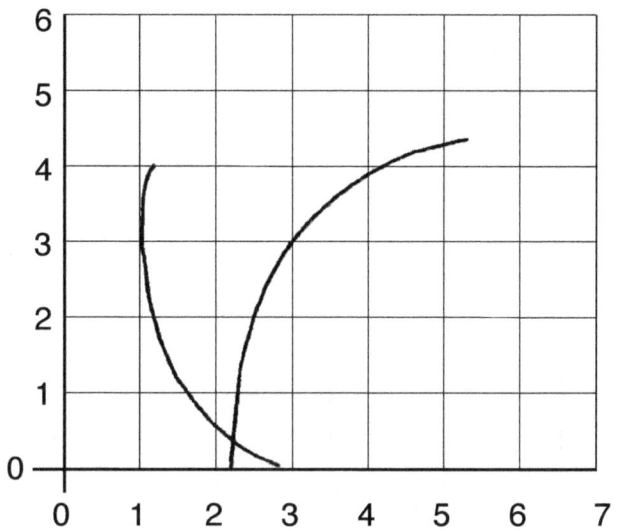

Identify the following on the grid:

gradient

co-ordinate

x axis

y axis

origin

point

intersection

positive slope

negative slope

graph

Co-ordinates

You will need two dice for this activity.

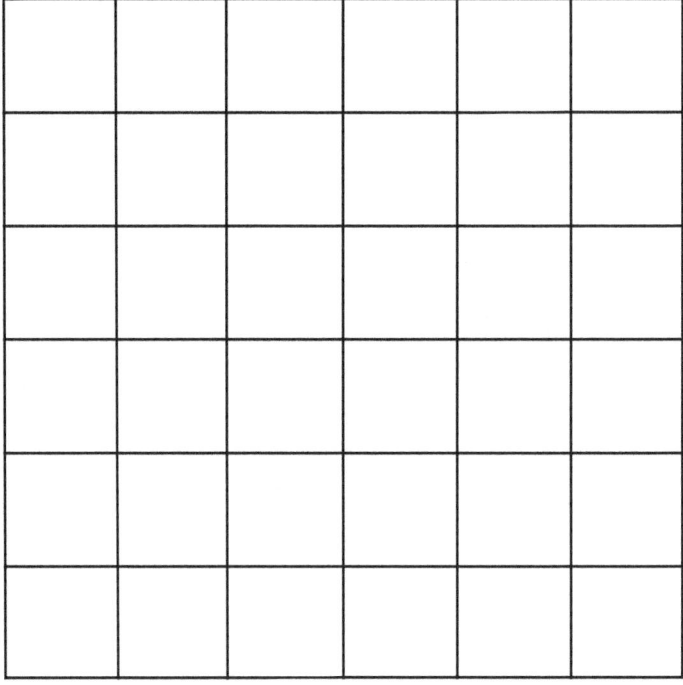

On the grid above identify

- the *x* axis
- the *y* axis

Number each axis from 1 to 6.

Throw two dice to identify a co-ordinate point and mark the position on your grid.

Repeat six times and join your points.

Find three co-ordinate pairs you did not use. Mark the position and write the co-ordinate pairs beside the grid.

Add-on
Work out the co-ordinate pairs for a rectangle with a perimeter of ten units.

Graphs 1

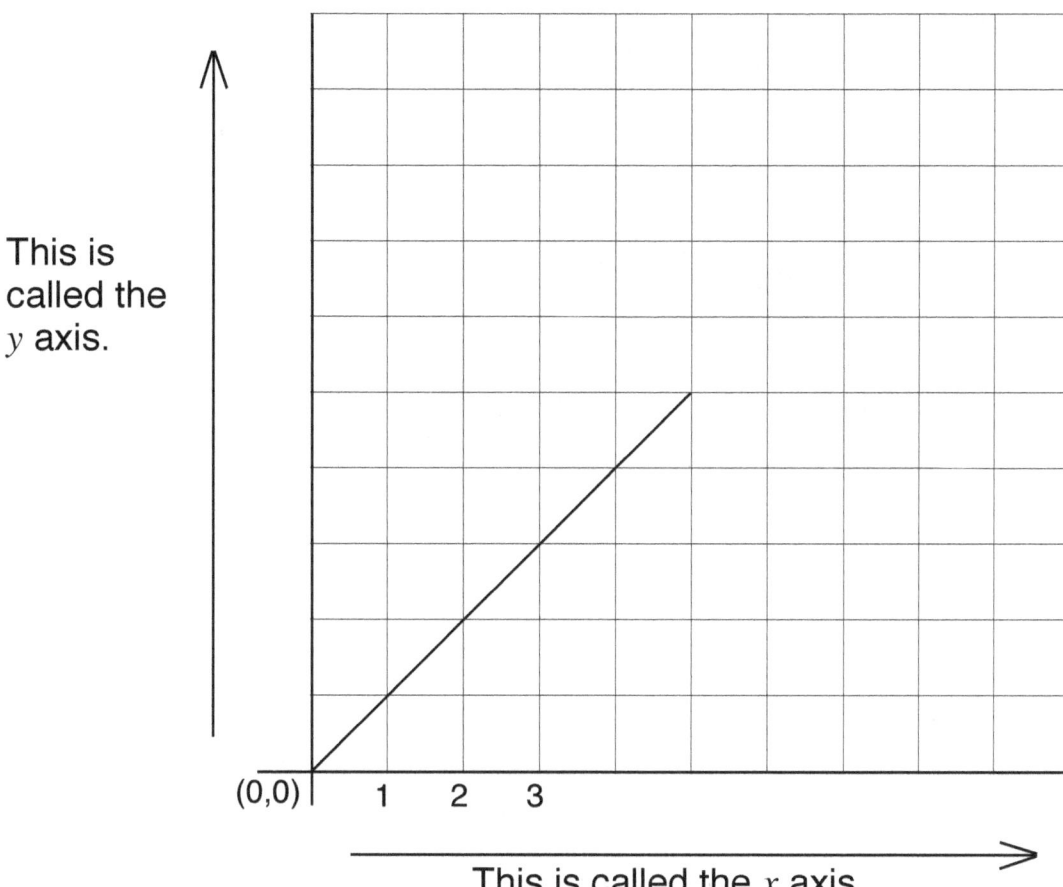

This is called the *y* axis.

This is called the *x* axis.

Number the *x* and *y* axes.

Continue the straight line graph.

Complete the co-ordinate table below.

Table of values

y	0	1								
x	0	1								

In this graph $y = x$

Add-on
Plot a graph of $x = 3$. Write values for *y*.

Graphs 2

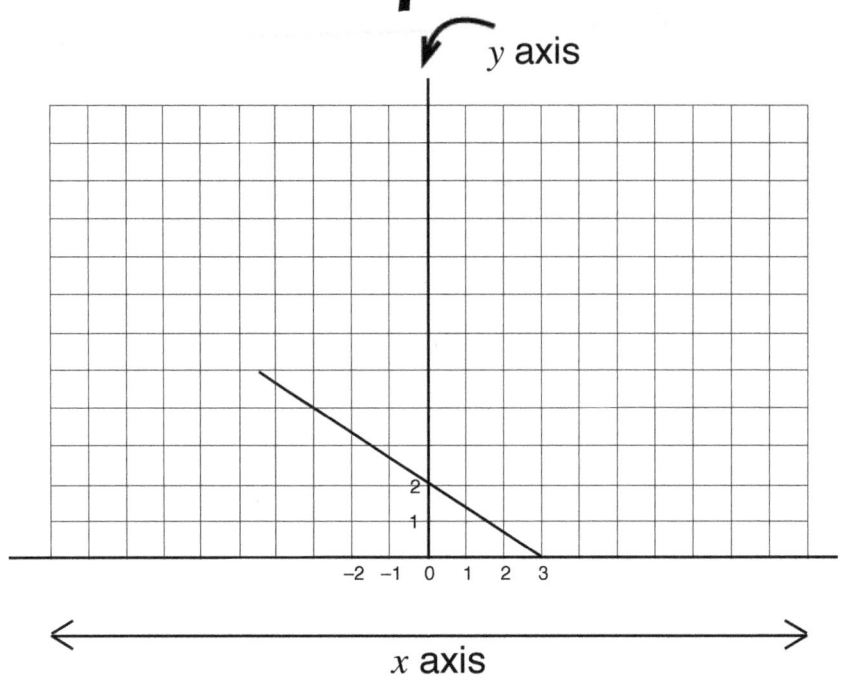

Number the *x* and *y* axes.

Continue the straight line graph.

Complete the co-ordinate table.

Table of values

x	−10	−9	−8	−7	−6	−5	−4	−3	−2	−1	0	1	2	3
y								4			2			0

Add-on
Continue the table of values up to *x* = 9

Graphs 3

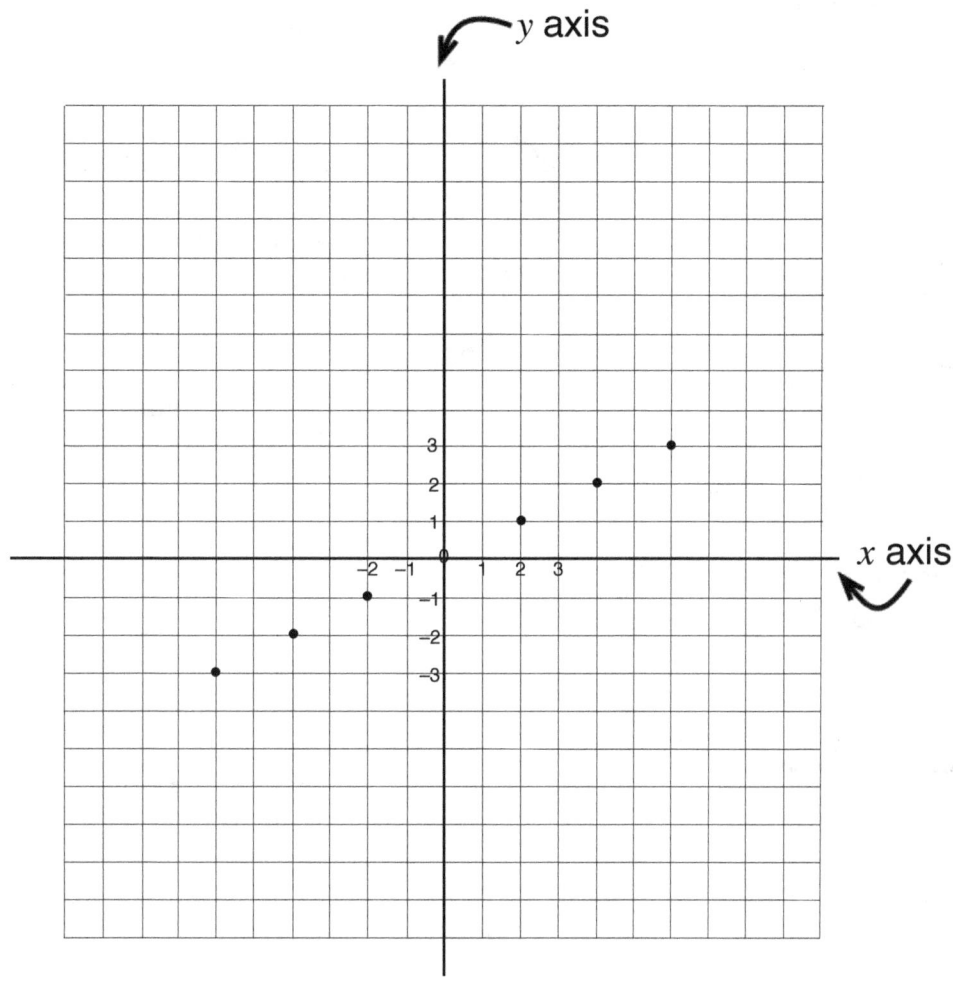

Number the *x* and *y* axes.

Continue the straight line graph.

Complete the co-ordinate table.

Table of values

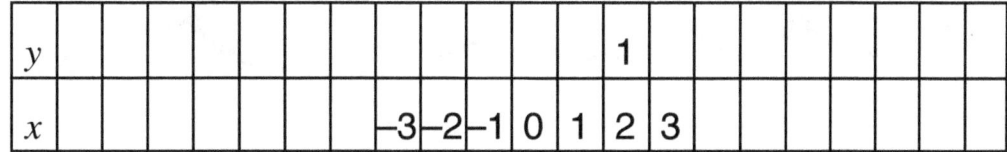

Add-on
Continue the table of values up to *x* = 8

Investigations

Find the missing values.

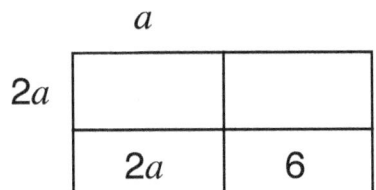

The length of a rectangle is twice as long as its width.
Its perimeter is 18 cm.
What is the length of its sides?

Draw a rectangle with a perimeter of $a + 4$ cm.

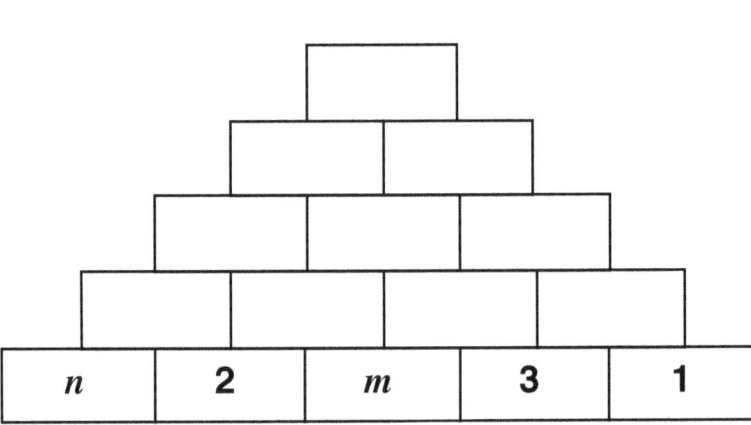

The length of a rectangle is 1 cm more than its width. The area is 20 cm. What is the length of its sides?

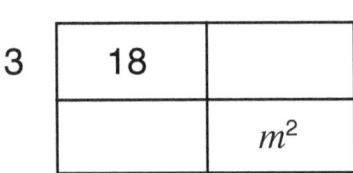

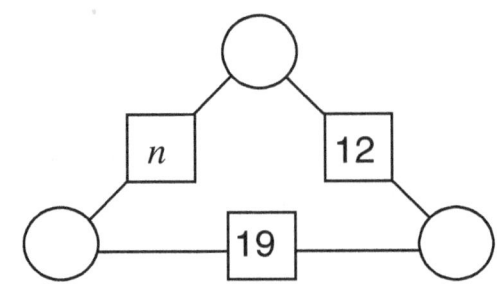

Check test 1

1. ☐ × 9 = 18

2. $2a + 1 = 11$ $a = ?$

3. Use letter symbols to show a number add 4.

4. $x = 2$ $4x - 6 = ?$

5. If $a \times b = 12$, what does $12 \div b = ?$

6. Simplify $2a + 3 + a + 1$

7. Solve $3x + 1 = 10$

8. If $x = 4$, what does $2x - 1$ equal ?

9. Continue the pattern 50, 39, 28, ?, ?

10. Continue the pattern 3, 6, 9, 12, ?, ?

    What is the value of the nth term?

11. x → ☐ ×2 → ☐ +1 → y $y = ?$

12. $(x + 3)(x + 1) = ?$

13. Write an expression to show twice a number add 6

14. If I have 4 times as many pennies as 2p coins and I have 18p altogether, how many pennies do I have?

15. A square has sides x cm. What is its perimeter?

16. Solve $2a + 7 = 13$

17. Does $(x + y) + 3$ equal $x + (y + 3)$?

18. If $x = -6$, what does $3x - 1$ equal?

19. Draw the graph $y = x + 1$

20. Complete the table:

x			−1	0	1		
y			0	1	2		

Check test 2

1. $6 + \boxed{} = 24$

2. $3n = 18 \qquad n = ?$

3. Use letter symbols to show 6 minus a number

4. $a = 3 \qquad 5a + 6 = ?$

5. If $a + b = 7$, what does $7 - b$ equal?

6. Simplify $4x + 7 - x - 2$

7. Solve $x + 3 = 10$

8. If $y = 5$, what does $2(y + 4) = ?$

9. Continue the pattern 5, 1, –3, ?, ?

10. Continue the pattern 12, 24, 36, 48, ?, ?

11. $x \rightarrow \boxed{\times 3} \rightarrow \boxed{-6} \rightarrow 9 \qquad x = ?$

12. $(y + 4)(y - 2) = ?$

13. Write an expression to show a number multiplied by 3

14. If I have 5 times as many CDs as I have tapes and have 6 tapes, how many CDs do I have?

15. A square has sides x cm. What is its area?

16. Solve $2a + 9 = 59$

17. Does $x + y = y + x$? Which law applies?

18. If $y = \frac{1}{2}$, what does $3y - 4$ equal?

19. Draw the graph $y = 2x$

20. Complete the table:

x			–1	0	1	2		
y			–2	0	2	4		

www.ingramcontent.com/pod-product-compliance
Lightning Source LLC
Chambersburg PA
CBHW081349160426
43196CB00014B/2704